YOUR KNOWLEDGE HAS VALUE

Silke Weishaupt

Conrad and Coppola and the Heart of Darkness Within:The Symbolic Value of Darkness in Heart of Darkness and Apocalypse Now

GRIN Verlag

Bibliografische Information der Deutschen Nationalbibliothek:

Die Deutsche Bibliothek verzeichnet diese Publikation in der Deutschen National-
bibliografie; detaillierte bibliografische Daten sind im Internet über http://dnb.d-
nb.de/ abrufbar

Imprint:

Copyright © 2003 GRIN Verlag GmbH
Druck und Bindung: Books on Demand GmbH, Norderstedt Germany
ISBN: 978-3-656-61962-8

This book at GRIN:

http://www.grin.com/en/e-book/24189/conrad-and-coppola-and-the-heart-of-dar-
kness-within-the-symbolic-value

GRIN - Your knowledge has value

Der GRIN Verlag publiziert seit 1998 wissenschaftliche Arbeiten von Studenten, Hochschullehrern und anderen Akademikern als eBook und gedrucktes Buch. Die Verlagswebsite www.grin.com ist die ideale Plattform zur Veröffentlichung von Hausarbeiten, Abschlussarbeiten, wissenschaftlichen Aufsätzen, Dissertationen und Fachbüchern.

Visit us on the internet:

http://www.grin.com/

http://www.facebook.com/grincom

http://www.twitter.com/grin_com

Silke Weishaupt

Universität Bayreuth

HS „Literature and Media Transformations"
SS 2003

Conrad and Coppola and the Heart of Darkness Within:

The Symbolic Value of Darkness in *Heart of Darkness* and *Apocalypse Now*

4

I. Introduction: A question of fidelity

"When a great artist in one medium produces a work based on a masterpiece in the same or other medium, we can expect interesting results" (E. N. Dorall: Conrad and Coppola: Different Centres of Darkness).

In his essay *The Rethoric of Narrative in Fiction And Film*, film critic Seymore Chatman observes that

'a lot of ink has been spilled in recent years on film adaptations of novels (...). Too much of the discussion has centred on questions of story content, with particular respect to 'fidelity', as if the source novel were some sacrosanct object whose letter as well as spirit the film had to follow.'[1]

He continues that this approach 'often leads to an unproductive prescriptivism that finds the film inadequate because it does not 'read' like the novel'[2]. It seems that John Milius and Francis Ford Coppola who both wrote the screenplay for the movie *Apocalypse Now*[3], had the same thoughts in mind when they decided to adapt Conrad's novel *Heart of Darkness* [4]-as Milius stated himself – 'in some shape or form'[5]. They certainly did not want to spill any ink and he also did not see the novel as a sacrosanct object. *Apocalypse Now* is not a conventional film adaptation of Conrad's novel since -at least at first glance- it does not pay particular respect to 'fidelity'; a Vietnam war movie does not seem to have much in common with a novel written in 1898 and dealing with colonialism. However, it is said that *HD* can be seen as the 'root' for *AN*, because 'a seventeen-year old John Milius heard his English reader, Irwin Blackter, extol the splendour of Conrad's novel *Heart of Darkness*'[6]. And if we take a closer look at the movie, the parallels to Conrad's novel become obvious. This essay will be divided into two major parts. The first one of will focus on the comparison of the plot and narrative structure of *HD* and *AN*. It will establish a general overview of the formal aspects of novel and film as well as of the similarities of characters appearing in both *HD* and *AN*. Special attention will be paid to the symbolic value of the plot of the story- the metaphorical meaning of darkness- appearing in both Conrad's novel and Coppola's movie and the question of how and why the screenplay-writers of *AN* applied Conrad's ideas on their film adaptation. The second part will be with special focus on Coppola's film adaptation of Conrad's novel. The analysis of several scenes

---

[1] Seymore Chatman, *Coming to Terms. The Rethoric of Narrative in Fiction and Film* (Ithaca: Cornel University Press, 1990), 163.
[2] Chatman, *Coming to Terms. The Rethoric of Narrative in Fiction and Film*, 163.
[3] In the following, *Apocalypse Now* will be abbreviated with *AN*.
[4] In the following, *Heart of Darkness* will be abbreviated with *HD*.
[5] Peter Cowie: *The Apocalypse Now Book*, (London: Faber & Faber, 2000), 2.
[6] Cowie: *The Apocalypse Now Book*, 2.

will pay special attention to details of techniques for visualisation and sound used by Coppola to depict the plot.

HD has not only inspired Milius and Coppola for their movie *AN*. It has served several other producers as an inspiration for their film. The Spanish filmmaker Manuel Aragon, for example adapted *HD* into film, interestingly, his film titled *Heart of the Forest* came to cinemas in the same year than *AN* came out. Both adaptations are not conventional ones as Conrad's novel is being transported into a different time into a different context. In *Heart of the Forest* is placed in the time of the Spanish civil war, and *AN* the movie this essay will pay special attention to- places Conrad's story right into the Vietnam War. The first question that arises to people's minds knowing both *HD* and *AN* is: Why is it that Conrad's story, playing in a different era 100 ago is so present in Coppola's movie.

II. Heart of Darkness and Apocalypse Now

1. The plot structure of Heart of Darkness and Apocalypse Now

On the surface it seems that Coppola's film is very different from Conrad's novel. In *HD* Joseph Conrad recreates a Congo journey that he himself has made as a young man. The story of *HD* is at least in part based on 'The painful experiences [Conrad] underwent during his brief employment by the Société Anonyme'[7]. It is narrated by its central character Charlie Marlow, a British sailor employed by a European trading firm as captain of one of their steamboats. The story takes place in the Belgian Congo at the turn of the twentieth century, a time when much of Africa, South America and Asia, having been divided up, were still under the control of a handful of European countries. Marlow is being sent on a mission in order to find and bring back Mr Kurtz, an ivory trader who disappeared into the interior of the jungle and never returned. As Marlow proceeds on his journey, the strange rumours of Kurtz's unorthodox behaviour fascinate him. As Kurtz seems to gradually engulf 'the atrocities of the other agents in his own horror'[8] his character grows in mystery and grandeur, and Marlow's journey soon becomes 'a series of impressionistic vignettes exposing the brutalities of colonial, and particularly Belgian colonial rule'[9]; Conrad severely

---

[7]   Richard Adams in: Joseph Conrad, *Heart of Darkness* (Harmondsworth: Penguin Books 1991), 105.

[8]   E. N. Dorall, 'Conrad and Coppola: Different Centres of Darkness' in: Joseph Conrad, *Heart of Darkness*, 'Backgrounds and Sources', ed. Robert Kimbrough (London: Norton 1988), 303.

[9]   Dorall, 'Conrad and Coppola: Different Centres of Darkness', 302.

6

criticises the corruptive power of colonialism and has Marlow express his contempt for expansionism:

> 'The conquest of the earth, which mostly means the taking it away from those who have a different complexion or slightly flatter noses than ourselves, is not a pretty thing when you look into it too much. What redeems it is the idea only.
> An idea at the back of it, not a sentimental pretence but an idea; and an unselfish belief in the idea- something you can set up, and bow down before, and offer a sacrifice to ...,[10]

It is exactly 'this idea only' that provides the context for both journeys in *HD* and *AN;* the idea in people's minds thinking that they have to gain control over people who are different to them, different because of their culture or their race or their religion. Conrad may have written his novel more than a hundred years ago, but the statement he brings across is transcendent. Francis Ford Coppola wrote synopsis for the film 'as much for his own consumption as for the public'[11] in which he explains his intentions behind the movie. The first thing he mentions is that *AN* is 'a retelling of Joseph Conrad's short classic *HD*. Set in Vietnam during the war in 1968.[12] This synopsis clearly stresses the parallels between the novel and the film. Coppola himself calls the American war in Vietnam 'to bring civilization to the ignorant millions'... the 'extension of mercantile colonialism'. For him, 'the horror and savagery lie not in the jungle, but in the American culture itself' The story of *AN* that is, as mentioned above set in the 1960ies in Vietnam and Cambodia, features a corollary to Marlow in Captain Benjamin Willard, a U.S. Army special forces operative assigned to go up the Nung River from Vietnam into Cambodia in order to 'terminate the command' of one Colonel Walter Kurtz who, he is told, has gone totally insane. Kurtz has taken his men over the border into Cambodia, where they are

---

[10]   Joseph Conrad, *Heart of Darkness*, ed. Robert Kimbrough (London: Norton & Company 1988), 10. All references to this book will be to this edition and will follow the quotation in parenthesis.
[11]   Cowie: *The Apocalypse Now Book*, 35.
[12]   Coppola continues the synopsis of *AN* as follows:
'It is the intention of the film- maker to create a broad, spectacular film of epic action-adventure scale, that however is rich in theme and philosophic inquiry into the mythology of war; and the human condition.
...As our protagonist travels through the insanities and absurdities of the American involvement in the war, he is more and more drawn to the jungle itself, its primeval mystique and immense power. It becomes clear that the American war 'to bring civilization to the ignorant millions' is merely the extension of mercantile colonialism and that the horror and savagery lie not in the jungle, but in the American culture itself, with its powerless [sic] technology and pop- culture.
...The story is metaphorical: Willard's journey up the river is also a journey into himself, and the strange and savage man he finds at the end is also an aspect of himself.....The intention is to provide the audience with an exhilerated [sic] journey into the nature of man, and his relationship to the Creation.
It is the hope of the film- makers to tell this story using the unique imagery of the recent Vietnamese War, its helicopter, disposable weaponry; as well as the Rock music, the drugs and psychedelic sensibilities. (Francis Ford Coppola in: Cowie, *The Apocalypse Now Book*, 35f.).

indiscriminately killing Vietcong, South Vietnamese and Cambodians. With the character of Kurtz, both Conrad and Coppola show us a man who was once very well respected. However, both men have decided to put themselves beyond the law of their commanders. Coppola's Kurtz, as he experienced his epiphany of the horror of war and the cultures he met, used to be an officer and a sane, successful, brilliant leader. Conrad's Kurtz, once he runs his own trading post single-handedly in the heart of the jungle, loses control and 'plung[es] into an abyss of moral degradation'[13]. Their hearts of darkness from within turn from the inside out. Their methods become 'unsound'(*HD*, 61), as they start using violence in order to control the natives. Conrad's Kurtz exploits them by trying to get as much ivory as he can form them. Coppola's Kurtz does not seem to have any method at all. Both Kurtzes let themselves worship by the tribesmen as demi-gods in order to keep them subservient to him. They use barbaric rituals held in his own honour:

> 'his nerves went wrong and caused him to preside at certain midnight dances ending with unspeakable rites. (HD, 50)

2. The Characters of Marlow, Willard and Kurtz

Both *HD* and *AN* are the story of Willard's and Marlow's journey up the river to Kurtz, their encounter and its consequences. Willard differs from Marlow in several ways, the most significant one being that he is sent on his mission specifically to kill Kurtz, unlike Marlow who is simply piloting others in the capacity of captain of a steamboat. Even though Willard holds the rank of captain, tying in with Marlow's occupation, he is not the captain of the boat which takes him and a party of others up the Nung river. However, Willard does communicate Marlow's fascination with Kurtz: 'I'd heard his voice on the tape and it really put the hook in me...'(SP, 18)[14]He continues reading Kurtz's dossier on his journey upriver and allows the Colonel's personality to 'penetrate and absorb his own'[15]. While both of them travel up a primeval river to fulfil their respective assignments, each speculates about the character of the man he is seeking, with the information each has pieced together about him. On their journey both characters are confronted with the negative aspects that are a result of the deeds of their home countries: The representatives of their own society are only

---

[13]   Gene D. Phillips, 'Darkness at Noon: *Heart of the Forest (1979)* and *Apocalypse Now (1979)*' in: *Conrad and Cinema: The Art of Adaptation*. (New York: Lang, 1995), 129.

[14]   John Milius and Francis Ford Coppola, *Apocalypse Now Redux- Original Screenplay*, ed Anahid Nazarian (New York: Hyperion 2000). All references to this book will be to this edition and will be referred to with the abbreviation SP and will follow the quote in parenthesis.

[15]   Dorall, 'Conrad and Coppola: Different Centres of Darkness', 303.

interested in one thing: fulfil their task- which is, in the case of *AN* war and in the case of *HD* ivory trade -to bring civilization to the 'untamed'. In both cases this is done through ruthless methods and without any respect towards the people. Marlow's description of the natives illustrates this brutality:

> 'Black shapes crouched, lay, sat between the trees leaning against the trunks, clinging to the earth... in all the attitudes of pain, abandonment and despair....They were dying slowly... they were not enemies, they were not criminals, they were nothing earthly now, nothing but black shadows of disease and starvation ...' (HD, 20).

Both Willard and Marlow reject the behaviour of their 'Companies' and by doing so show themselves as being morally superior to them. Willard describes the mission he is given by the U.S army as ridiculous: 'Charging a man with murder in this place was like handing out speeding tickets at the Indy 500' (*SP*, 15) Their physical quest gets them into a country strange and unknown to them. However, the psychological aspect of their quest plays the more essential role in both book and film as both questers start putting into question the methods used by their 'companies' and start their own, internalised quest.

3. The rivers as symbols for the inner journey

The image of the river is referred to in both book and film again and again. The rivers symbolize the inner journey and the inward changes of the characters:

> 'Going up that river was like travelling back to the earliest beginnings o fthe world, when vegetation rioted on the earth and the big trees were kings. An Empty stream, a great silence, an impenetrable forest.' (*HD*, 35)

AN adopts Conrad's basic concept of the river,

> 'resembling an immense snake uncoiled, with its head in the sea, its body at rest curving over a vast country, and its tail lost I the depths of the land'. (*HD*, 16)

Willard talks about 'a river that snaked trough the war like a circuit cable... plugged straight into Kurtz.' (*SP*, 6). Marlow also remarks: 'The river was there- fascinating-deadly- like a snake.' (*HD*, 14) Both characters are confronted with the 'overwhelming realities of this strange world of plants and water and silence' (HD, 36), as the river leads them deeper and deeper into the heart of darkness. The depiction of the river in *AN* is very significant and will be discussed in the sequence analysis of the film in a later chapter.

9

4. The Heart of Darkness within: the metaphorical meaning of darkness in the novel. [16]

"In the interior you will no doubt meet Kurtz"(HD, 22).

As Marlow starts his account of his journey to rescue Kurtz, the 'darkness' seems to stand for the goal of that journey, the unknown. But, we gradually begin to wonder, does this centre of darkness have geographical, metaphysical , or psychological significance? [17] In his essay *Heart of Darkness: "Will and Wilderness"*, Nic Panagopoulos proposes that 'the jungles of the Congo can be seen as a metaphor for a society where men have been reduced to beasts through the loss of that ethical and rational order which their religious beliefs used to provide.' He applies the theory of Schopenhauer's 'will'–the dark primeval force through which human beings are 'intimately allied to the wilderness of life'. 'Marlow is not just discovering the truth about colonialism in going to Africa'[18],, and Willard is not just discovering the truth about war in going to Vietnam: both protagonists also discover the truth about themselves and life in general. 'Conrad's novel reflects the post- Darwinian idea that at the heart of man is not a metaphysical soul but a blind and instinctive natural force, the object of which is to maintain the individual at all costs. Metaphorically speaking, just like Africa was an uncharted region on a map for Marlow in his boyhood, man's centre has 'ceased to be a blank space of delightful mystery ... It had become a place of darkness'(*HD*, 12).

Therefore, the jungle which is depicted in *HD* can be seen as a metaphor for the heart of darkness which lies in each of us, the 'inclination of evil that lurks in each of us'[19], on which centres lies Kurtz. As Marlow tells us, Kurtz 'lacked restraint in the gratification of his various lusts'(*HD*, 57). What Conrad suggest trough his novel is that, 'if someone like Kurtz lacks strong ethical principles of his own, the superficial restraints which civilized society places on one's moral behaviour, represented by the

[16] Conrad's symbolic use darkness in the novella has been discussed by many critiques and could be discussed as an essay topic of its own. Therefore the meaning of darkness will be discussed rather shortly. However, as it forms the main motif in both book and film and will therefore be relevant for the analysis of the movie, a basic understanding of the concept is necessary.

[17] Anthony Fothergill, *Heart of Darkness- Open Guides to Literature* (Milton Keynes: Open University Press 1989), 5.

[18] Nic Panagopoulos, 'Heart of Darkness: Will and Wilderness' in: *Anglo- American Studies: The Fiction of Joseph Conrad. The Influence of Schopenhauer and Nietzsche*, (Frankfurt a. M.: Lang 1998), 77.

[19] Phillips, 'Darkness at Noon: *Heart of the Forest (1979)* and *Apocalypse Now (1979)*', 127.

guardians of Law and Order, are gradually forgotten in the isolated, barbaric atmosphere of the wilderness.'[20] Marlow says that the wilderness

'...had whispered to [Kurtz] things about himself which he did not know, things of which he had no conception till he took counsel with this great solitude- and the whisper had proved irresistibly fascinating. It echoed loudly in him because he was hollow at the core.' (*HD*, 57)

HD suggests that not only are the forces of civilization and progress weaker than the 'darkness' they are attempting to overcome but that the civilizing impulse itself may be no more than a sublimation of the same instinctive force it is pitting itself against. This means that the civilizing impulse is nothing more than what everyone of us living in a civilized society constantly has to do with themselves but at the same time is struggling against: being in control of- or hiding- the instinctive force of darkness within our subliminal self.

Despite his enormous intellectual gifts, Kurtz is morally corrupted when the wilderness whispers to him things about himself he did not know because he has lost those illusions which *HD* regards as 'man's sole defence against demoralization in life'[21]. Marlow must somehow rescue Kurtz from the darkness of nausea and doubt if he wants to salvage his own faith in the power of civilizing illusions:

'I tried to break the spell , the heavy mute spell of the wilderness that seemed to draw him to its pitiless breast by the awakening of forgotten and brutal instincts...' p 65.

AN is a darker rendering of *HD*. *HD* rather is the story of how to survive the approaching horror.[22] The novel still has a positive force in the character of Marlow- he is 'a moral force personified'[23] and remains intact and succeeds in conquering the darkness. In *AN*, unlike Conrad's novel there is only darkness. The character of Willard is morally unstable. As mentioned earlier, the war Vietnam can be seen as an extension of mercantile colonialism; however, Willard's confrontation with war is more life-threatening than is Marlow's confrontation with the colonial rule in the Congo.. Whereas Marlow moral character is strong enough to resist the temptations of the jungle. Luis Greiff notices that

20   Phillips, 'Darkness at Noon: *Heart of the Forest (1979)* and *Apocalypse Now (1979)*, 127.
21   Panagopoulos, 'Heart of Darkness: Will and Wilderness', 95.
22   Dorall: 'Conrad and Coppola: Different Centres of Darkness', 309.
23   Dorall: 'Conrad and Coppola: Different Centres of Darkness', 308.

'Willard offers little improvement over Kurtz as potential moral center of the film. The audience first sees him on leave, holed up in Saigon in a condition of physical and spiritual depravity. He recovers when given a mission, but then enters a long, passive period on the PBR.'[24].

Whereas Marlow has the mission to save Kurtz from himself, Willard gradually turns into a second Kurtz himself. After having killed Kurtz, however, he 'rejects the option … of replacing Kurtz as savage king'[25]

5. The narrative structure

Coppola also orientates himself on the narrative structure of Conrad's novel. At this point, I would like to refer to Peter Brooks and his observation that *Heart of Darkness*

> 'poses…central questions about the shape and epistemology of narrative. It displays an acute self-consciousness about the organizing features of traditional narrative, working with them still, but suspiciously, with constant reference to the inadequacy of the inherited orders of meaning. …it pursues a reflection on the formal limits of narrative, but within a frame of discourse that appears to subvert finalities of form. …it engages the very motive of narrative in its tale of a complexity motivated attempt to recover the story of another within one's own, and to retell both in a context that further complicates relation of actors, tellers, and listeners.'[26]

Conrad wants to overcome the self- imposed restrictions of the novel. Therefore the text self-consciously addresses the question of its own narrative process as it can be seen in the following passage:

> The yarns of seaman have a direct simplicity, the whole meaning of which lies within the shell of a cracked nut. But Marlow was not typical (if his propensity to spin yarns be excepted), and to him the meaning of an episode was not inside like a kernel but outside, enveloping the tale which brought it out only as a glow brings out a haze, in the likeness of one of these misty halos that sometimes are made visible by the spectral illumination of moonshine. (*HD*, 9).

If 'moonshine' is interpreted in its metaphorical meaning foolish or nonsensical talk, one could say that Conrad is concealing himself behind Marlow's moonshine. Just like Conrad unmasks the conventions of the narrative, Coppola, in his reading of Conrad's novel, unmasks the conventions of the war- epic and subverts the conventional cinematic techniques for war-films. One could say that *AN* poses central questions about the shape and epistemology of war- movies. It displays an acute self-consciousness about the organizing features of war- movies.

---

[24] Louis- K. Greiff, 'Soldier, Sailor, Surfer, Chef: Conrad's ethics and the Margins of Apocalypse Now' in: *Literature- Film Quarterly Vol. 20/ 3*, 1992, 190.
[25] Greiff, 'Soldier, Sailor, Surfer, Chef: Conrad's ethics and the Margins of Apocalypse Now', 190.
[26] Peter Brooks, 'An Unreadable Report: Conrad's *Heart of Darkness*' in: *New Casebooks- Joseph Conrad, Contemporary Critical Essays*, ed. Elaine Jordan (London: Macmillan 1996), 67.

HD is a framed tale in which a first narrator introduces Marlow and has the last word after Marlow has fallen silent. The novel has two narrative points of view: that of the unnamed narrator on the cruising yawl Nellie docked in the Thames estuary and that of Marlow who tells his story as a fresh water sailor, navigating into the heart of darkness. In his essay film critic di Giuseppe points out that those different points of view function as a means of 'drawing a distinction between narrative voice and text implication'.[27] The unnamed narrator represents the novel's bias 'prone to an exhaltation of imperialism' whereas Marlow's tale 'shapes the material into dramatic form' and allows the reader to see a very imperfect imperialism through text implication by undermining the narrative voice . Marlow remarks: 'This also... has been one of the dark places of the earth' (*HD*, 9). Film critic Di Giuseppe notices that *AN* also as two narrative plots: Whereas 'Conrad distinguishes the unnamed speaker's grand narrative from Marlow's tale- spinning, Coppola separates the narrator's 'slant'[28] which is Captain Willard's voice-over, from the 'filter' of text implication, which is the eye of the camera. In other words, Willard's narration actually rather represents Conrad's unnamed narrator, whereas the camera eye is given 'exclusive rights to text implication', as it filters and subverts the grand narrative with 'Marlow- like critical punctuation'.

6. The question of point of view

The function of the camera concerning point of view is of great interest to this essay of comparison between book and film. The point of view of a film is rather abstract and global [29](Monaco, 195- 205). 'The moving camera has an ethical aspect, the question of point of view is at the heart of this ethical code' (Monaco, 208).As mentioned above, the camera eye is given 'exclusive rights to text implication'. Most films, like most novels, are told from an omniscient point of view. We see and hear whatever the author wants us to see and hear. However, unlike in novels 'a first person mode is not possible in film because the difficulty is that we see what is happening as well as hear it. In the novel, in effect, we only hear it'(Monaco, 208). In film there is

---

[27] R. di Giuseppe, 'Imperialism as Entertainment: Coppola's Adaptation of *Heart of Darkness*' in: *Quaderni di lingue e letterature Vol. 20*, ed. Università degli Studi Verona, 1995, 93-103.
[28] di Giuseppe, 'Imperialismas Entertainment' (Verona:1995),
[29] James Monaco, *How to Read a Film: The World of Movies, Media, and Multimedia,* (Oxford: OUP 2000). All references to this book will be to this edition and will follow the quote in parenthesis.

always the presence of the image and therefore there is always the element of description.

Therefore in a movie it is more difficult to imply, than it is in a work of fiction, that 'a given account of past events is being presented from the subjective point of view of one of the characters. In *AN* Coppola works with voice- over narration., comments form the off where the viewer only hears the voice of the protagonist suggesting an inner monologue. as when Willard recalls in his voice- over commentary his initial misgivings about carrying out his secret orders to assassinate Kurtz when he finds him.'[30] A film audience is always conscious that it is watching what is being dramatized in flashback on the screen- not through the eyes of the character who is narrating the events in question- but through the eyes of the camera. The voice of the character who is recalling the events in question is added in the soundtrack as a voice-over in order to retain the subjective dimension of these memories. As the flashback unfolds on the screen, the character –Willard- gives subjective reflections on the events. However, the viewer still does not have the sense that he is seeing the flashback from the point of view of the character who is retelling the event.[31] Graham Greene once explained that

> 'One cannot tell a story from the single point of view of one character in a film as one can in a novel…You cannot look through the eyes of one character in a film…'

Greene continues that it is true that the central character remains on the screen more than anyone else in the movie, and his comments are often there on the sound track 'But we still don't see others completely from his point of view as we do in the novel.'[32] Whereas in *HD* Marlow frequently communicates to the reader his subjective reaction to the episodes from the past he is narrating, the filmgoer watching *AN*

> 'never grasps the extent to which Willard, the narrator of the film, is profoundly touched by Kurtz's tragedy in the movie, since many of the sage reflections about Kurtz's life and death which Marlow makes in the book are simply not in the film.'[33]

As a result, one cannot show darkness in a film the same way it is depicted in the novel. Whereas a book lives through words and through words only a film lives through the image.

---

30   Phillips, 'Darkness at Noon' in *Conrad and Cinema: The Art of Adaptation*. 137.
31   Phillips, 'Darkness at Noon' in *Conrad and Cinema: The Art of Adaptation*. 138.
32   Quoted by Phillips, 'Darkness at Noon' in *Conrad and Cinema: The Art of Adaptation*. 138.
33   Phillips, 'Darkness at Noon' in *Conrad and Cinema: The Art of Adaptation*. 138.

III. The Language of Film: Signs and Syntax[34]

Before I start with the analysis significant scenes and sequences of *AN*, it is necessary to define specific terms concerning the language of film. As a basis I will refer to James Monaco's book *How to Read a Film*, particularly to chapter three, which gives a good overview on the language of film.

1. The syntax of film: Mise-en-scène and Montage

"Setting up a scene is as much an organizing of time as of space. The aim of this is to discover in film a psychological reality that transcends physical, plastic reality." *[Monaco, p. 174]*

The syntax of film is the systematic arrangement of cinematic language. Its major difference to written or spoken language systems lies in the fact that film syntax not only deals with the linear aspect of putting together words to form phrases and sentences but that it includes spatial composition, which is both the development in time and in space. In film criticism, the modification of space is referred to as "mis-en-scène", whereas the modification of time is called "montage" (Monaco, 172).

1.1. Mis-en-scène

This French phrase, literally meaning "putting in scene" is concerned with the basic aspects of the syntax of the static film frame and particularly with the limitations the frame imposes and, as the frame determines the limit of the image, the composition of the image within the frame. What is decisive here is the filmmaker's attitude towards the limit of the frame and the composition he or she chooses which can either be a closed form, where the image of the frame is self-sufficient, or an open form, where the audience is subliminally aware of the area outside the frame. Additionally and of great importance is the relationship of the movement within the frame and the movement of the camera. Here, special attention has to be paid to certain filmic codes of the composition of different planes within the frame and the relationship between the compositional factors in separate planes, namely the plane of the image in relationship to the geography of space surrounding it, for example a plane parallel, horizontal, vertical or diagonal with ground and horizon, an oblique or a symmetric composition.

---

34   Even though specific signs appearing in the film cannot be ignored, I will limit the film analysis mainly to the syntax of film and therefore the following description of terms will also be limited to the syntax. Specific terms of film syntax will be presented rather shortly, as discussing them in detail would go beyond the scope of this essay. Therefore, the analysis of *AN* assumes that the basic facts on film syntax are familiar to the reader. However, the elements of film syntax will be explained in more detail in the course of this essay simply because they will be referred to as they appear in the analysis of different scenes of the movie.

Furthermore the relationship of the arrangement of subjects/ actors within the limited space of the frame is of great importance, with regard to proximity and proportion like foreground/ background. All of these are important subcodes as they affect the psychology of human perception. Other factors that need to be paid attention to is the intrinsic interest of colour, form and line and, in addition, the modification all those elements through lightning codes, for example highlighting that calls attention to details- hair and eyes most often, backlighting that can dominate a subject or sidelighting causing a dramatic chiaroscuro effect. (Monaco, 183- 195).

A very important element of mis-en-scène is the so-called diachronic shot, which is concerned with dynamic qualities. Factors that come into play here are distance, focus, angle, movement and point of view, with the latter being of special interest for this essay, as in film this factor is very different to the point of view of a novel. Distance is concerned with the shot- distance, that varies from full shot, medium shots and close-ups. The focus can range from a deep, relatively sharp to a shallow or soft focus. The change of focus which can be either a follow focus to keep a moving subject in focus or a rack focus that changes attention away from one subject and toward another is the element that connects the codes of composition with those of movement. The factor of angle is concerned with the relationship between the camera and the subject on three different axis: the pan or vertical axis i.e. the angle of approach, the tilt or horizontal axis, i.e. the elevation of shot and the roll, the horizontal that parallels the axis of the lens, which is however, very seldom used. The camera not only revolves around the three axis but is also moved form one point to another. Tacking shots move the viewer physically into the scene and both the spatial relationships among objects shift but also the perspective of the audience. In contrast we have the zoom where the camera does not move and therefore relationship amongst the objects and the relationship of the viewer remains the same. The last shot variable is the point of view. It needs no further discussion at this point, because it has already been mentioned in the preceding chapter.

1.2. Montage

The meaning of the French term Montage seems more suitable for describing the process of putting together the shots of a film as a film is seen as being constructed rather than edited. Whereas "cutting" or "editing" the terms used in the U.S. only suggest a trimming process, "montage" rather implies a building action, a working up from the raw material. Whereas mis-en-scène is marked by a fusion of complexities, montage is can be summarized in a rather short way, as there are only two ways of putting two pieces of film together: one can put them end to end or one can overlap them. Concerning the latter, different techniques can be used such as double exposure, dissolves or multiple images. Those techniques can be seen as the punctuation devices of cinema and will be discussed in further detail later on.

These techniques are used to connect scenes an a certain way in order to create so-called "syntagmas", units or narrative elements that have meaningful relationship with each other and that can exist within shots as well as between them. (Monaco, 216-225). Any montage occurring in a film can be seen as 'a dialectical process that creates a third meaning out of the original two meanings of the adjacent shots'(Monaco, 216).What has to be considered here is the ever- shifting and complex syntax of film through the relationship of film segments towards each other. Each film segment either is: autonomous or it is not, chronological or not, descriptive or narrative, linear or not, continuous or not and organized or not.(Monaco, 224).

As mentioned earlier in this chapter, punctuation devices are techniques used to connect different scenes in a certain way. They can be compared to punctuation devices in written language. There are different types of film punctuation. such as the fade that calls attention to the ending or the beginning, by fading out or fading in. The most important element of the punctuations in cinema is the dissolve which superimposes fade out and fade in. It is the one mark that mixes at the same time that it conjoins them. (Monaco, 225).

IV. Film analysis with special focus on the implication of darkness

The following analysis of *AN* will pay special attention to the filmic methods used by the director Francis Ford Coppola to depict darkness- in a metaphorical way. In AN, the viewer gets confronted with the darkness of the lunacy of war and the darkness inside every human heart.

The analysis is based on the DVD *Apocalypse Now- Redux*[35] As further support, the screenplay will be used. [36]

---

[35]   Zoetrope Studios, *Apocalypse Now Redux* , 2002, playing time 195 min, DVD the time will be added in parenthesis.
[36]   John Milius and Francis Ford Coppola, *Apocalypse Now Redux- Original Screenplay*, ed Anahid Nazarian (New York: Hyperion 2000). All references to this book will be to this edition and will be referred to with the abbreviation SP and in this chapter will follow the quote in parenthesis.

1.The beginning

The beginning of *AN* differs in many ways to the beginning of Conrad's novel. From the first second on with the beginning sequence of the movie Coppola achieves the impression of death and destruction through the use of montage and music. The very opening shot of the film is a jungle scene 'burst[ing] into a bright red-orange glob of napalm flame' (*SP*, 1). Accompanying this picture is the soundtrack of 'The Doors' singing 'this is the end, my friend', not only suggesting a subversive stance as the beginning announces itself as the ending but also signalling the film's circular movement. The 'framed tale', is not missing in Coppola's adaptation as *AN* provides a 'creative imitation of the Conradian frame' (footnote??)- a disembodied voice as was Marlow's own on the darkened Thames- to begin and end the film. The frame narration is done by Jim Morrison, lead singer of The Doors singing the song 'The End'. The beginning announces itself as the ending just as in *HD* the initial scene on board the Nellie occurs, chronologically, long after the events recounted in Marlow's yarn. The song creates a certain apocalyptic atmosphere and functions to prepare the audience for the action that will follow.

In the next frame, the viewer sees and hears a helicopter. The frame tightens to what appears to be the hub of the propeller. However, when the frame opens one becomes aware that what is seen is a superimposition of images: The picture dissolves and what becomes visible is a blinking eye over the rotating propeller which is really only a ceiling fan turning above a recumbent figure. A 'syntagma'- a meaningful relationship is created through the montage of those images; the blending of propeller, ceiling fan and eye implies an eye- witness narrative 'but the camera's eye more than suggests that this eye-witness is unreliable'[37]as the first appearance of Willard's face is filmed upside down. Here, we encounter a character that seems to be very different from Marlow. We are confronted with a man obviously in a deep psychological crisis. The close- up of Willard's face dissolves into a shot of the hotel room, the helicopter and ceiling fan are blended with images of explosions of bombs. This implies Willard's psychological destruction through his earlier experiences in the war. He seems to be inwardly torn apart, side- lightning of the close- up of his face stresses Willard's psychological unstable condition as it appears in half- shadow. This is stressed even

---

[37]   Di Giuseppe, 'Imperialism as Entertainment', 100

more in the following diachronic shot, where Willard's face starts spinning around as the camera rotates and thereby imitates the movement of the ceiling fan and helicopter.

What immediately follows this frame is the movement of the camera away from Willard's face: it pans and it filters different items lying on a table next to his bed: photographs, letters, cigarette papers, a glass- supposedly filled with whisky- a spoon, little white packets and a gun. Those objects are used as filmic codes to sketch a shorthand biography of Willard. The items fall into 'two distinctly opposed categories or mental functions: memory and oblivion' [38]. The former is symbolized by the photographs and letters and the latter by the cigarette papers- a representation of marijuana- the glass of alcohol- and the spoon and the packets - metonymically representing heroin. The strongest vehicle of oblivion is represented by the gun. What the camera tells us is that Willard's situation is dominated by oblivion more then by memory. He is a solider traumatized by his experiences in the war and unable to return and adapt to the civilized world which he is therefore trying to escape from through alcohol and drugs.

Willard makes his first utterance in the next frame (00:04:07). 'Saigon ... shit. (SP, 2). When he mentions he is 'waiting for a mission' (SP, 2) the camera shows a close- up shot of his face with the shadow of the rotating ceiling fan on it. Foreshadowing the events to come. This foreshadowing is even stronger in the next shot (00:05:49). We see Willard as a shadow figure on the left side of the film frame performing 'some sort of martial art' (SP, 2), which is an allusion to the scene on the Kurtz compound at the end of the film, namely the simultaneous ritual slaughter of the caribou and of Willard killing Kurtz. The scene climaxes with Willard fighting his own image in the mirror. Here, the camera takes the position of the mirror so that we have a Willard staring directly at us, implying just as Marlow suggest in *HD* that Western man is his worst enemy.

2. River sequence: The Mekong Delta

Just as in HD, the river- as symbolizes the inner journey of the questers – is constantly referred to in *AN*. When Willard talks about the river for the first time he calls it ' a river that snaked through the war like a circuit cable... plugged straight into Kurtz,' (SP, 6). And indeed: the river 'snakes' through the whole movie as it is depicted in many scenes. At the beginning of the river journey there is a shot of the Mekong river Delta at dusk (00:19:00); (SP, 14-15). As the small PBR navy boat

---

[38]   Di Giuseppe, 'Imperialism as Entertainment', 100.

moves away from the dock and the camera we get a frame shot from above overlooking the river that is still relatively wide but surrounded by the dark shadow of the jungle on both sides. The scene blends into another shot where the boat approaches the camera. As the viewer cannot see where it is moving to, the scene arouses the feeling that the crew is moving into the unknown. Very significant is the frame composition: the line of the horizon cuts the screen in half: above it is the mystic yellow light of the sky at dusk and underneath it the blackness of the water on which the boat is barely visible. With the next cut, the boat moves away from the camera into the dark. The impression that is created is that the mission leads Willard into the unknown. He obviously does not know what to expect: 'I really didn't know what I'd do when I found [Kurtz]' (SP, 15)

3.The air raid of Vin Drin Dop (00:24:00-)

"Our culture looked down upon the Vietnamese because they were more simple than us, just as Europe... looked down on the Africans. Believing ourselves superior , we had a lot of trouble dealing with the discovery that we are not." (Worthy: 24)

In this scene, the fascination of war and its lunacy is depicted with full force. The scene starts with an extreme full shot of the helicopters - 'as they deploy into a formation and move through the frame, performing 'almost a dance of dragonflies'(SP, 35); they look magnificent in the sky' (SP, 36). Accompanying the scene is the muted electronic music of the soundtrack that makes helicopter gunships seem like living creatures. The soundtrack also stresses the particularly dehumanising aspect of the war in Vietnam: the fact that the killing is not face to face but done by machines with the push of a button. The relation between man and machine can be seen as sexual one as the machine extends man's power and therefore making him 'super-phallus'[39]. The air raid scene is dominated by fast cuts between the helicopter bomber pilots including the mad Colonel Kilgore.......firing bombs on a Vietnamese village accompanied by the radio voices of the crew- 'Outstanding, Red Team; get a case of beer for that' or 'Nice shot, Bill' (SP, 41) with close- ups of the devastatingly violent consequences these machines have on the bodies of human beings. What seems like a farce is Kilgore's order to play Wagner's *Ride of the Valkyries* (00:36:00) over the loudspeakers to intimidate the enemy and exhalt his troops. The booming loudspeakers and the noise of the helicopters preclude all dialogue. The apocalyptic overtones are enhanced by the contrasting note of this celestial chorus which accompanies the legion of helicopters

---

[39]   Saul Steirer, „Make Friends with Horror and Terror: Apocalypse Now' in *Social Texts Vol. 3* (Durham: 1980), 114-122.

advancing at sunrise. The viewer is given 'a postmodernist version of the classical *deus ex machina* descending providentially on the scene.' [40] Throughout the scene Coppola blends the pictures of the spectacular air ride with close- views on Willard. He is 'watching the spectacle' (SP, 40). He does not take part in the action but rather is in deep thought reflecting about the madness he witnesses. Just like him, the audience sees the dark side of man, however it gets manipulated by the visual treatment of the whole scene and it seems the pictures and music are so strong that even Willard's critical comment at the end might fail to get his message across:

'If that's how Kilgore fought the war...I began to wonder what they really had against Kurtz. It wasn't just insanity and murder. There was enough of that to go around for everybody.' (SP, 59)

5.Du Lung Bridge (1:36:00)

For Willard and his crew going upriver with their PBR, the Du Lung Bridge at the border between Vietnam and Cambodia is the last 'civilized' station 'Beyond it there was only Kurtz' (SP, 121). This scene embodies most totally the madness and the pointlessness of the military operation in Vietnam: during daytime the bridge is being destroyed by the Vietcong in order to be rebuilt by the American soldiers during the night. The scene is set in the night. As the crew approaches the bridge on the river, we get a full view of it from the distance. The bridge in the centre of the dark night frame is lit up by bright fires burning and sparks from welding (SP, 120). There are flares arcing trough the night sky above the bridge. Darkness dominates the whole scene. The visual quality of the scene evokes 'unreal futility' [41] Coppola puts the viewer in a surrounding of total disorientation. Willard leaves the boat with Lance who is on drugs- he dropped acid (SP, 121) and wears camouflage. His experiences of the war in the jungle make him turn more and more savage. He looks ahead fascinated by the pyrotechnics, commenting 'It's beautiful.' (SP, 121).Soldiers are running around in the darkness. The disorder of the whole scene is supported through the soundtrack: disharmonious synthesizer music accompanies the dark scene that is occasionally lit by parachute flares. The camera follows Willard and Lance who is looking dreamily at the 'phantasmagoric strings of lights the smoke, the fires' (SP, 124). They walk through the chaos and disorder of the scene trying to find the commanding officer. However, they are not able to find him- obviously there is no commanding officer. They are lit

---

[40]   Di Giuseppe, 'Imperialism as Entertainment', 102.
[41]   Steirer, 'Make Friends with Horror and Terror: Apocalypse Now', 119.

occasionally by the battle in the background. The next frame is a close up of Willard's face observing the disorder and chaos of the scene in disbelief.

The scene has parallels to *HD*, where Marlow stops his journey upriver as they 'crept on, towards Kurtz' (HD, 39). He comes upon 'a hut of reeds' (*HD*, 29) that has been left. The only tie to western civilisation is the book he finds there: *An Inquiry into some Points of Seamanship* written by a man called Towson. Both the bridge and the hut mark the last point before the arrival at Kurtz's compound. From now on there are no more ties to western civilization as there is nobody who represents its values.

5. River sequence: The arrow attack

As the crew moves on, the surrounding becomes more and more threatening. Mist swells up and around the river as the boat moves into an obscure fog (SP, 157); (2:14:00). Throughout the scene we only catch glimpses trough the moving fog, of all the crew members on the PBR searching the shoreline (SP, 158).Chief, the captain of the boat wants to stop it as he cannot see anything. The whole crew is disoriented. The camera angle focuses on Lance. He has his face painted in a kind of tribal camouflage. He is turning savage and has obviously lost his ties to western civilisation. Lance utters a loud scream that also reminds of a tribal ritual. Willard's voice over comment underlines the atmosphere of the whole scene: 'He [Kurtz] was close ....I couldn't see him yet, but I could feel him, as if the boat were being sucked up river and the water was flowing back into the jungle. What follows now is the arrow attack (2:16:00). Arrows whiz around the boat from out of the jungle. It seems like the crew is not getting attacked by humans as there are none visible- but by the jungle itself. This event has been taken over by Coppola directly and without any changes to it from Conrad:

> 'Sticks, little sticks were flying about...whizzing before my nose, dropping down below me...Arrows, by Jove! We were being shot at!'

This sequence in the film retains its links to its source trough the death of Chief as in *HD* the helmsman is killed by the arrows.

6. The Kurtz Compound

Ever since the Du Lung Bridge sequence, the whole pace of the movie has been slowing down. Before the arrival at Colonel Kurtz's compound, there is another significant river scene:

(2:19:00) The first shot is set at night. The camera moves on board the PBR and focuses on the shore that is being lit up with burning torches . It then moves its focus to the faces of the remaining crew as they take in this sight. (SP, 162). The frame of this picture speaks a very strong language: The camera perspective is from the boat. The picture is framed by the black of the jungle. The only source of light is a patch of the yellow sky at dusk. In the foreground we see the silhouette of Lance standing at the back of the boat, moving in a slow motion Tai Chi or some kind of tribal dance. Again, this stresses that the savage side of him has taken over. The image of the frame gets darker and darker creating a claustrophobic, threatening feeling. The boat moves away from the camera and disappears in the darkness.

The scene dissolves into the shot of the PBR on the river by day. The boat passes rows of skulls, flaming torches and dead bodies impaled on poles. The boat moves towards the camera in the fog surrounded by the black jungle the picture dissolves into an different perspective.

The river becomes wider and the fog disappears. Willard and his crew are at the goal of their journey upriver. The crew passes hundreds of Montagnard natives 'body and faces painted in white, of the most savage nature' (SP, 163) The surrounding has no more connections to western civilisation.

'In entering Kurtz's outpost in the wilderness, Willard has equivalently stepped back into lawless, prehistoric age where barbarism holds sway. The compound, then, becomes a graphic visual metaphor which reflects Kurtz' gradual descent into primitive barbarism.'[42]

When Willard walks around on the compound with Lance he is caught by a group of Montagnards. He is being turned upside down and dragged in the mud. During the whole scene the frame is almost a black screen. We can only see some shadow figures while the camera rolls upside down. This symbolizes the inversion of values on the Kurtz compound where the wild and untamed that are considered to be wrong by western civilisation, have taken over the rule. (2:30:40)

The next scene (1:31:00) shows Willard's first encounter with Kurtz. The camera follows him entering the temple. Again, this whole scene is dominated by darkness. Kurtz's first words appear out of the dark. As the camera approaches towards the direction of the voice, Kurtz's contours become visible. The camera focuses on his face, however the back of his bald head is all the viewer and Willard can see, the rest is covered in darkness. The darkness of the scene stresses the topic of their conversation: Kurtz's 'unsound methods' (SP, 177) and Willard's classified mission as an assassin to

---

[42] Phillips, 'Darkness at Noon' in: *Conrad and Cinema: The Art of Adaptation*, 139.

terminate Kurtz's command. Only at the very end of the scene, Kurtz's face appears in the light (2:25:28), however half of it is still covered in darkness.

The scene of the second conversation with Kurtz (2:50:00) is also dominated by darkness. Kurtz tells Willard about his encounter with horror:

> 'Horror has a face. And you must make a friend of horror. Horror and moral terror are your friends. 'You have to have men who are moral, and at the same time, who are able to utilize their primordial instincts to kill without feeling, without passion. (SP, 186)

Mostly all we see is a dark frame. All there is Kurtz's voice out of the darkness. In between there are close ups of his face lit only from one side. The scene also includes close ups of Willard's face. Significantly, his face is also in half shadow implying his inner conflict as on the one hand he has seen the face of horror himself- in the form of war- but on the other hand wants to put an end to Kurtz's unsound methods.

The final scene (2:58:35), is probably the most intense and breathtaking one of the whole movie. It combines a very strong visual quality with an intense soundtrack. Willard decides to compete his mission: 'Everybody wanted me to do it. Him most of all. I felt like he was up there, waiting for me to take the pain away.' (SP, 189). The full shot shows Willard's face emerging out of the muddy water of the river. The scene resembles a rebirth and stresses the mystical meaning of Willard's mission. Willard's appearance out of the swamp is accompanied by the sound of lightning. Willard enters the temple. We see Willard's face – he wears camouflage- in close up, approaching the silhouette of Kurtz. The following action shows Willard's ritual killing of Kurtz. Coppola uses parallel montage showing the scene of a ritual slaughter of a water buffalo intercut with the scene taking place inside the temple: Willard brings the machete down and starts hacking away at Kurtz, hitting him first at the shoulder, then all over (SP, 191). Simultaneously the natives are slashing a knife into the back of the water buffalo. This parallel montage evokes associations with sacrifice rituals. The scene implies that the actual sacrificial object is Kurtz. Willard redeems Kurtz from his god-like role as he is no longer able to free himself. As Kurtz falls on the floor, the frame becomes unstable as the camera starts moving to the left and the right, up and down. Willard's killing of Kurtz is performed in a dark surrounding. Only fragments of the action are visible. Kurtz's last words are 'The horror. The horror.' (SP, 192). The intensity of the scene is supported by the soundtrack which ties in to the very beginning of the film. The song 'The End' by the Doors builds the frame narrative with which the film closes.

After having killed Kurtz, Willard leaves the temple. As he is standing at the top of the steps the viewer can only see one half of his face, the other half is in the darknes. Coppola uses this lighting to stress Willard's inner conflict. Willard has to decide whether to become Kurtz's predecessor or to go back to civilisation. However, the steps out of the shadow, drops his machete and passes through the crowd of Montagnards who have also dropped their weapons. On his way he takes Lance with him and takes him back to the boat.

V. Conclusion

With *AN* Coppola has created an unconventional but in my eyes very successful adaptation of Conrad's novel. As shown in this essay, the movie takes over the basic structure of *HD*, concerning plot and narrative structure but also with respect to the metaphorical meanings implied in Conrad's work. Coppola has successfully achieved the task to place Conrad's critical world view into a contemporary surrounding. Both works severely criticise the society and politics of their time. Both authors imply the hypocritical ideals, the materialistic values and the superficial behaviour of their time and of the people that live in it. Through this, the double standards of society are revealed. Both main characters begin to put into question the methods used by their 'companies' and start their own internalised quest that leads them to the dark side of man. The actual physical journey that they both undertake at the same time, which is their journey to Kurtz is also a metaphor for their psychological journey into the inner self. The character of Kurtz symbolizes the idea that there is a dark side that lies in each of us and that society corrupts man: 'All Europe contributed to the making of Kurtz'(*HD*, 50), just like Coppola's Kurtz is a product of the American society. The General even stresses this in his conversation with Willard:

> Well, you see, Willard…in this war, things get confused out there. Power, ideals, the old morality, and practical military necessity. But out there with these natives, it must be a temptation to be God. Because there's a conflict within every human heart between the rational and the irrational, between good and evil. And good does not always triumph.' (SP, 13)

The restraints that these societies place on one's moral behaviour are superficial. Both Kurtzes symbolize the lack of strong ethical principles in society. Once one is isolated from them, these principles are forgotten.

Coppola's film is worthy to stand as a new creation beside the Conrad novella from which it derives.[43] In *AN* Coppola succeeds in translating the symbolic value of darkness that Conrad employs in the novel. The transformation of a literary work into film requires the employment of specific filmic means like frame composition, lighting or soundtrack. Coppola makes full use of those means in order to put the whole complexity of Conrad's novel onto the screen. The visual and acoustic processing of the film certainly leave a lasting impression on the viewer. Therefore the film often seems to speak a much stronger language than the novel. *AN* is a darker rendering of *HD*. *HD* rather is the story of how to survive the approaching horror.[44]The novel still has a positive force in the character of Marlow- he is 'a moral force personified'[45] and remains intact and succeeds in conquering the darkness. In *AN*, unlike Conrad's novel there is only darkness. The character of Willard is morally unstable- he seems to turn into Kurtz himself. It is uncertain what happens to him after he has fulfilled his mission: 'Unlike Conrad's world, however, Coppola's America does not offer the stable consensus standards or ideals against which the actions of Kurtz [...] seem horrible.[46] What Conrad warned against and in some measure provided for has arrived: Coppola's version of darkness leaves no way out.

"...I had a little green paperback of Conrad's 'Heart of Darkness' in my pocket, filled with notes and markings. I just naturally stared referring to it more than the script, and step by step, the film became more surreal and reminiscent of the great Conrad novella." (Francis Ford Coppola in the Introduction of: APOCALYPSE NOW REDUX- THE SCREENPLAY, Zoetrope, New York: 2000).

---

[43]   Dorall: 'Conrad and Coppola: Different Centres of Darkness', 309.
[44] Dorall: 'Conrad and Coppola: Different Centres of Darkness', 309.
[45] Dorall: 'Conrad and Coppola: Different Centres of Darkness', 308.
[46]   William M. Hagen, 'Apocalypse Now (1979): Joseph Conrad and the Television War', in: *Hollywood as a Historian; American Film in a Cultural Context*, ed. Peter C. Collins (Lexington 1983), 245.

VI. Works cited

Primary sources

Books

- Conrad, Joseph. *Heart of Darkness*. Ed. Robert Kimbrough. London: Norton & Company, 1988.
- Milius, John and Francis Ford Coppola. *Apocalypse Now Redux- Original Screenplay*. Ed. Anahid Nazarian. New York: Hyperion, 2000.

Film

- *Apocalypse Now Redux*. Dir. Francis Ford Coppola. DVD, running time 195 min. Zoetrope Studios, 2002.

Secondary sources

- Adams, Richard. *Joseph Conrad- Heart of Darkness*. Harmondsworth: Penguin Books, 1991.
- Brooks, Peter. 'An Unreadable Report: Conrad's *Heart of Darkness*'. *New Casebooks- Joseph Conrad, Contemporary Critical Essays*. Ed. Elaine Jordan. London: Macmillan, 1996.
- Chatman, Seymore. *Coming to Terms. The Rethoric of Narrative in Fiction and Film*. Ithaca: Cornel University Press, 1990.
- Cowie, Peter. *The Apocalypse Now Book*. London: Faber & Faber, 2000.
- Di Giuseppe, R. 'Imperialism as Entertainment: Coppola's Adaptation of *Heart of Darkness*'. *Quaderni di lingue e letterature* 20 (1995): 93-103.
- Dorall, E. N. 'Conrad and Coppola: Different Centres of Darkness'. *Joseph Conrad- Heart of Darkness*. Ed. Robert Kimbrough. London: Norton, 1988.
- Fothergill, Anthony. *Heart of Darkness- Open Guides to Literature*. Milton Keynes: Open University Press,1989.
- Greiff, Louis- K. 'Soldier, Sailor, Surfer, Chef: Conrad's ethics and the Margins of Apocalypse Now'. *Literature- Film Quarterly* 20/ 3 (1992):188-98.
- Hagen, William M. 'Apocalypse Now (1979): Joseph Conrad and the Television War'. *Hollywood as a Historian; American Film in a Cultural Context*, ed. Peter C. Collins. Lexington: 1983.
- Monaco, James. *How to Read a Film: The World of Movies, Media, and Multimedia*. Oxford: OUP, 2000.

27

- Panagopoulos, Nic. 'Heart of Darkness: Will and Wilderness'. *Anglo American Studies: The Fiction of Joseph Conrad. The Influence of Schopenhauer and Nietzsche*. Frankfurt a. M.: Lang, 1998.

- Phillips, Gene D. 'Darkness at Noon: *Heart of the Forest (1979)* and *Apocalypse Now (1979)'*. *Conrad and Cinema: The Art of Adaptation*. New York: Lang, 1995.

- Steirer, Saul. 'Make Friends with Horror and Terror: Apocalypse Now'. *Social Texts Vol.3*. Durham: 1980.